THE NON-WINE SN
Part 4

By Dennis Valder

July 9, 2014

CONTENTS

ISBN-13: 978-1500113544
ISBN-10: 1500113549

DRIVING THE OLD PINTO!

Sometimes you have to pull the old Ford Pinto out of the garage, fill up the tank and just go somewhere! Anyplace, just go!

This book is for both the wanderlusts and couch potatoes who are interested in finding something different to drink, other than the 'Old Favorite' that they have been sipping for decades.

A few million years ago, my wine interest was only what I could sneak out of my mother's cupboard without getting caught. Yes, that didn't last long. I would not recommend adding water to the wine bottle and expect that the old lady isn't going to figure it out. It was Mogen David. How would anyone know? She must have been psychic!

Fast forward through the end of the Ice Age and I landed at the L.A. County Fair in Pomona in the 1980's, where they were exhibiting many international wines.

To use the words of the cowboy in *Blazing Saddles*, "I didn't know there would be so many!"

Having been told by others that white wine was a fall from grace, I tasted a few red wines and left the hall with the impression that Southern Comfort on the rocks wasn't so bad after all.

Red wines? Who drank that stuff? Even worse, who was the poor slob that was so thirsty that he decided to drink fermented grapes? And how did he sucker all of those other people into believing it was worth trying?

"Look at this, I found this barrel of grapes that has gone bad and it smells to high heavens and I'm going to dip my cup in and try the stuff. After pushing all the floaties away from the top, or course. Oh, wait, those are flies."

Definitely a hard sell!

And now I am writing a book about wine. I suppose stranger things have happened.

My wine guzzling did not start at a winery in Junction, Texas; but, this story starts there.

Junction, Texas? Where is that? Junction is in between "I'm lost" and "Why does anyone live here?" Or if you are really curious, milepost 456 on Interstate 10 about one hundred miles north of San Antonio.

No, I didn't drive all that way from Houston just to pick on the locals. They are actually really nice folks, especially in light of the fact that they didn't boot me out of town when I took all of their wine.

I was motoring along the I-10 on a road trip from Los Angeles when my gas gauge and stomach paired their needles, telling me a stop would be advised. Having had the experience of Junction before on another jaunt across the endless state of Texas, the idea of dried up over-battered chicken didn't seem appealing. I knew I could survive until the next town, maybe even to the Flagstop Cafe near Bourne.

Pushing the old vehicle wasn't on my itinerary; so, I coasted off the freeway looking for a gas station. At the end of the off ramp there was a sign, "Junction Rivers Winery" pointing 'that way.'

Right! Junction, 'Out in the Middle of No Where Texas' has a winery? Should I humor myself with a drive-by or just fill up the tank and mosey out of town?

I looked at my watch and thought, "What the hell, it has to be entertaining!"

After losing more money to the prehistoric dinosaurs (gasoline), I drove down the main street in search of this distraction. The signage wasn't perfect as I got turned around in the beginning, but I finally parked in front of the Tasting Room.

"Open on Thursday," the sign on the door read, and guess what? It was Thursday!

I found an oasis in the desert.

Jeanie Brosius King, winery owner, great cook and wonderful tour guide welcomed me, along with her staff.

She fed me and dragged me around the winery operation, while I steadied a glass of wine. Life is wonderful, but this couldn't be Junction, Texas!

Predominately a red wine operation, all of their wines are made in-house in stainless steel vats in limited production, around 500 cases a year. It is an extremely clean facility that impressed me with their manufacturing process and focus on detail. No, I didn't get any production secrets, but that might be on my next trip. I'll weasel out a few, if I can.

Oh, and the winery is a major award winner, too! Like a hunting lodge with bagged trophies on the wall, the numbers of awards are impressive. Junction, Texas? Hard to believe.

I highly recommend their Cabernet Franc and Ruby Cabernet. Both were 2011 vintage, though I am sure that all of the years are wonderful. In fact, I was forced to lighten her burden of inventory buy purchasing a few cases, 'for the road!'

Contact information:
www.junctionriverswinery.com
210 N. 6th Street
Junction, Texas 76849
(325) 446-2600

I suppose I could either give credit or a disclaimer to Jeanie for the idea of writing this book. While I was there, I signed one of my other books for her, while she had her husband, Dr. Joe King, sign his book, "Animals." If you love animals, buy the book.

In order to find some of the wonderful unknown wineries in person, you have to take a chance. I am glad I took the chance with this little town out in the middle of nowhere.

You can't always be that lucky, but that doesn't mean you can't enjoy the adventure.

Later on, I will explain about how Texas saved the French wine industry. No, the French do not want to talk about it.

WHERE TO FIND GREAT WINES ON THE ROAD

My mother, bless her little heart, said I had ants-in-my-pants.

Hey, there might be a winery on the other side of the hill! The only way for me to find out would be to drive over and see. It is my personal belief that the automobile was created to let me discover the world. I also believe the growth of wineries, especially in the United States, is due to the horseless carriage. Why would you pony up in search of another winery if you couldn't haul any of the loot back?

Since I started this book with the golden treasure of finding Junction, Texas, I'll tell you about what used to be the Golden State of California. Yeah, I know, every wine book has to blather on about California. The previously golden state has some nice wineries and most folks have heard about them. You have to give them a lot of credit for how much they have done in the grape-squeezing business.

For California, the Thomas Winery in Cucamonga started it all in 1838. Oh, here come the seven horses of hell after me for slander! I have found more than one winery up in the Napa area that swears they started it all. They didn't.

Nope, sorry, the monastery of the Thomas Brothers needed something to quench their thirst while trying to convince the local inhabitants that the Great Spirit only talked through them. All the other wineries will just have to accept Second Place.

Though many California wineries have started in the years after the Thomas Brothers, many have also failed to make it. Eventually, so did the Thomas Brothers, as well as the famous Virginia Dare, well-known in California's history. It was named after the first child born in the Americas in the Roanoke Colony, North Carolina. As you recall, everyone mysteriously disappeared and no one knows what happened to them.

Cucamonga Valley was once the largest private vineyard in the world with Secondo Guasti's Italian Vineyard Company taking top honors. Like so many other wineries in the region, that once massive wine operation is now covered up with houses and freeway interchanges.

So much for your history lesson, now let's get back to wine!

My wife and I were in the town of Temecula, north of San Diego, one week before New Year's. Let's just say it was a while back. We had stayed at a local hotel, rather not impressive; but, I did see an old historic hotel trying to stay alive on one of the main streets. Like throwing a bone to a dying dog, I wanted to see if it was worth staying there if we decided to check out the many wineries in the area.

In the hotel lobby, one side was the registration, while the other side was a wine tasting room. I parked my wife in the wine bar, while I went about discovering the creaking boards that covered the floors upstairs. While it was interesting, the idea of a common bathroom and furniture that was turn of the century, yes, the other century, did not appeal to me as much as I thought. Yes, it was quaint.

Downstairs my wife was discovering the mother lode! Curry Vineyards Winery, with the owner, Charlie, chief grape-squeezer, bottle-filler and occasionally the label applier showing off what I later found to be a wonderful list of red wines.

Now, to go back in history, I had always been a white wine drinker. Red wines gave me nasty headaches if I drank more than half a glass. Who drinks half a glass of wine?

Charlie Curry showed me the error of my ways concerning reds. By the time he was finished with us (me); my vehicle was loaded up with many more cases than I want to admit. Let's just say this road trip was rather expensive, but not because of Charlie. His competitors in the area helped. How there was room for our luggage I do not know, but somehow we were able to drag everything back to Houston. Oh wait, there was room, but you'll find about that later in New Mexico.

Charlie has a great range of red wines and just recently started dabbling in the white stuff. No, not that white stuff, white wine. It might take a while, but he will figure it out. I didn't jump up and down about the chardonnay, but then I'm tired of that old brand. His sauvignon blanc is worth picking up a few bottles and some are resting comfortably in my wine cellar. He recently told me he is up to 1,000 cases a year. Not bad for an old surfer dude-turned-grape-stomper.

He no longer has the little place in the dilapidated hotel. Now he has a nice place around the corner at:

Curry Vineyards
41946 5th Street
Temecula, CA 92590
(909) 821-1282
curryvineyards@aol.com

If you happen to be in the area, check him out. What I like about his red wine is that I do not get a headache from it. (Yes, I did weasel the secret of that out of him while he was recovering from surgery; but no, I'm not going to tell you!)

The other remarkable thing about his wine is the taste consistency. With some red wines, there is a strange taste with the first pour. An odd aftertaste; I'm not sure how to describe it, but if you ask the wine snobs in the room, they will explain it. With Curry Wines I don't get that odd taste or the headache.

If you drop in on him, continue my research to see if you get the same opinion. Good luck on trying to squeeze more secrets from him. He is as healthy as a horse now.

Any sommelier, that's French for Wine Snob, can tell you about Napa Valley wines. There are thousands of books on the subject and this is not one of them. This book is on how to find the treasures, not about running around in the hallowed halls of the great north vineyards. If you happen to be up there, take the Wine Train. Other than that, you are on you own.

As my wife and I labored out of Charlie Curry's wine tasting room with our cases of wine, we had to visit a few others that I was aware of, but she was not.

Around the corner is Lorimar Vineyard's tasting room and it is worth stopping by. They also have a big spread on Anza Road, but I have not been there, only the place in Old Town. Sip and stroll through a few of their wines, too.

More wine! Geez, where would we put all of this stuff?

If you are adventurous enough, the whole region is dotted with wineries and tasting rooms.

Like someone may have told you when you were getting too frisky, "Get a room!" There is nothing that kills a good wine buzz faster than a police car in your rearview mirror!

*

As we motored out of California, always in search of another winery, we stopped in Deming, New Mexico. (Yes, I know we went through Arizona, but I haven't found a shockingly good winery there.)

I knew about the Luna Rosa Winery and I wanted to share that experience with my wife. Though I may have been unimpressed with Arizona wines, I have found a few decent ones in New Mexico, of all places. Yes, New Mexico, the Land of Enchantment, or so the license plates say. Enchantment? I guess New Jersey's, 'The Garden State,' was already taken.

My first experience with New Mexico wines was in Albuquerque, many years ago. There is a restaurant/wine tasting room/bar, the St. Clair Winery and Bistro, just off I-40. I was staying at a nearby hotel and decided it might be better than the fast food joints that dotted the area.

I was still nearly a virgin in the world of wine experience, so I was easily impressed when not only did they have decent wine, but they also had pretty good food. They may be the largest winery in the State-- or they told me they were. I didn't personally count all of their rows of grapes, but it is possible that they are.

I tipped my toe into the water, not willing to jump in too deep. I tried this wine and that wine, finally selecting a few bottles to bring home, possibly stumbling back to my hotel room.

You have to be willing to try wine at the strangest places if you are going to get out of the rut of liquor store choices. An area I will try to avoid in this book, though admittedly there are wines available about everywhere, if you look hard enough.

If you happen to be in the area, here is their address and info:

St Clair Winery & Bistro
901 Rio Grande Blvd NW
Albuquerque, NM 87104
(505) 243-9916
www.stclairwinery.com

Where was I? Oh, yeah, Luna Rosa Winery in Deming. It is another extraordinary find and very much worth the stop, though getting there, even though you can see it from the freeway, can be annoying.

Before I tell you about their wines, I have to tell you a funny story.

Sylvia D'Andréa is a wonderful cook! If you can plan your trip at a time when she is catering an event, or she has just finished one, you will be in luck. She feeds me!

How much better can it be than tasting good wine and good desserts?

My wife and I were sitting comfortably on our stool when she asked if we would like a piece of tiramisu. I'm not sure why anyone would say, "No" but, since I had already benefited from her cooking in the past, I was drooling before the words were out of her mouth!

Then she explained this might be the most expensive tiramisu known to humanity. More drooling, while my trembling hand was extended in anticipation.

As her story goes, she had catered an event the day before and one of the desserts was this piece of 'pick me up' as the Italian translation means. While she was making it she looked around and found a bottle of brandy that was lying around. You know, just a bottle of something that had, "Brandy" on it.

Later, her husband, Paolo, inquired about his bottle of Gran Duque d' Alba.

"I don't know what you mean," she replied.

"My best bottle of brandy is missing. Someone has been in my liquor cabinet. It has a red wax seal on it."

"The Alba stuff? Oh, I used it in my tiramisu."

"What? That was a hundred dollar bottle of brandy! Thank you very much for treating our customers to the best you can get."

Well, it sounds a lot funnier when Sylvia explains it, but I was still begging for a second piece when she finished the story. Can't waste old tiramisu, you know. That would be a sin!

Their wines are very nice, both the reds and the whites. The selection should be good for just about anyone. I like their Pinot Grigio and Chenin Blanc for whites and all of their reds. Don't drink the Sangiovese, that is MINE!

Well, maybe only one bottle.

They also have a little store that has the standard paraphernalia with things you just have to see to appreciate. Quite a bit of it is locally made.

If you are in the area, here is their location:

Luna Rosa Winery
3710 W. Pine Street
Deming, NM 88030
(575) 544-1160
www.lunarosawinery.com

Knowing there is always enough room for another case of wine (or two) we found a place for it in the back along with Charlie Curry's and a few other Temecula wines as we departed the Luna Rosa Winery. The taste of Sylvia's tiramisu lingering on my taste buds.

"On the road again..." a song that might be permanently tattooed on the inside of my skull, was playing in my mind. Now we had to get home, there was not enough space for more wine.

("Panic Attack!" I just checked my wine collection- that is what you are seeing on the front of this book- and I am down to only one bottle from Luna Rosa. A 2004 Nini. How I have allowed that blunder to go undiscovered, I do not know. If you are headed to Houston from Deming, I will give you my shopping list.)

Once upon a time I took a job in Rochester, New York for the summer. I don't need to tell you how different the winter is in Upstate New York compared to Houston, Texas.

In the past, I had been a student at the University of Rochester, taking only summer classes related to optics, a big industry in the area. Or it was back then.

I had heard about their wine industry hugging the many Finger Lakes. Everything I heard was bad. The comparison always seemed to have the term 'Boone's Farm' in the description, and not in a good way. At the time I had not taken much interest in wine, no matter what region it was from.

But, as I had this four-month opportunity in Rochester, with weekends pretty open, I decided to drive around the Finger Lakes and check out the scenery.

After stopping in at the Glenn Curtis Air Museum in Hammondsport, I decided to try one of the wine tasting rooms, knowing it would be nothing but rotgut.

Sometime in between my summers learning about optics and this job, the Finger Lakes Wine Region took a serious turn.

A certain gentleman, Dr. Konstantin Frank, changed all of that. His story is very interesting and worth knowing, if you happen to live in that part of New York.

The simple and short version is that the Finger Lake wines are remarkable. Like any group of grape squeezers, some of the wineries are fantastic, some are interesting and some might be considered 'entertaining.' That is my nice way of saying I wouldn't try it twice.

Since you cannot go from 'here' to 'there' with water all around the place, you have to drive around the Finger Lakes. That is annoying; so, you have to plan your trip. There are so many wineries in the region that picking a specific lake and staying with it is my recommendation.

You can try another lake on another trip. There are many nice places to stay, with hidden little restaurants nearby.

Is it a coincidence that there are four weeks in a month and there are four different lakes? I shouldn't have to tell you that I have nearly planned a month for you. Don't forget there are about ninety wineries in the area. Let's see, ninety wineries divided by four weeks, divided by two days. Yep, 11.25 wineries per day. Write to me and tell me how the .25 winery went.

With all the wine tasting, the cracker snacking and beautiful scenery, maybe you need to make that a two month plan.

I have many of the Finger Lake wines in my wine cellar, though I admit the inventory is slowly diminishing. There is only one reason for that. Yes, I have been known to drink wine once in a while. Perhaps I should come up with a worthless reason to stock up.

A great way to start the trip is with a wine map; but, that is not necessary. You can check out this website:

www.fingerlakeswinecountry.com

They have all the information that you will need and I cannot find a single thing to complain about concerning their website. Very few internet wine maps even come close.

That is not the same as motoring down the road and finding a hidden winery someplace. One that only sells at their winery, but it is worth the effort. If you are trying to find a reasonable excuse to take a wine road trip, you might be reading the wrong book. You take that road trip for a reason. The adventure! (Make sure your arms are in the air when you say that!)

It's just like not eating at chain restaurants when you are away from home, finding a small winery nestled in the turn of the road is part of the fun. Isn't that why you bought that old Pinto in the first place: to wear it out before it falls apart?

What I have found remarkable are the Finger Lake Rieslings. Sometime in the past, I tried this sugary purple water that was labeled 'Riesling' and after that one taste I mentally wrote that nasty stuff off. It is the fastest way to turn you into a diabetic in one day. I'll pass.

Try the Finger Lake Rieslings; you will be very surprised. They do not have the syrup I was expecting and most of the wines in the region (maybe all of them) have a sweetness scale right on the bottle! I wished the other wineries would do that, but I think the New York Board of Grape Pickers and Stompers requires the information.

Of course! It is New York! What was I thinking?

They have outpaced California in who can regulate the most. I heard they have even standardized the color of toilet seats.

Have another glass of wine, and all of it will go away.

Just after the Ice Age, when that same weirdo was drinking the fermented barrel of rotten grapes, an enlightened philosopher/poet/statesman, Eubulus, around 365BC is quoted as saying, "Three bowls of wine is the right amount." You gotta like the guy, even if he somehow got mixed up with what he wanted to be when he grew up. How can you be a statesman, a philosopher and a poet in the same body?

Now I don't know how big the wine bowls were back in those days, but if you are going to go wine tasting, calm your little butt down and don't drink too much. Nobody seems to have a dedicated driver when they need one in the middle of the Finger Lakes. So use your head. After the second gallon of wine, you can't remember whether it was the Heron Hill winery that had a great red with the moon on it or was it the one with the rooster on the label. If that is the case, your taste buds are worthless, too.

Many of the wineries either have hotels connected, or are nearby. Use them.

*

If you haven't noticed, most of my winery searches start with a rolling vehicle.

I was driving along Interstate 57, southbound in Illinois, the State of Perpetual Road Construction, when my car magically turned off the freeway after it noticed a sign advertising a winery. What a shock! How can I ever get rid of a car that knows me so well?

After a bit of what turned out to be dirt road driving (my GPS didn't know there was a paved road available!) I found the Blue Sky Winery in Makanda, Illinois.

A very nice place, with some very nice wines. Having a friend who lives on Blue Sky Drive in another state, I figured I could at least buy a bottle with his address on it.

Another two cases of wine later, I was motoring away after trying most of their wines. They have a very, very nice Norton as well as a Viognier that is worth looking into. If you buy any of their wines, some have labels that are so artistic that you need to find a reason to keep the empty ones. Doesn't work for me, but I know some people who would cherish them for years.

It was more than surprising that Illinois had a winery, let alone a decent one. The view upon the hilltop is amazing! Imagine a stereotype Italian villa with grape vines as far as you can see, and that is Blue Sky Winery. They have cabins, or as they like to call them, 'suites,' available nearby and the room rates are extremely reasonable.

The people who ran the place were probably more business-like than the normal fun-loving winery managers I was used to, but their wines make up for it.

If you are in the area, here is their information:

Blue Sky Winery
3150 S. Rocky Comfort Rd.
Makanda, IL 62958
(618) 995-9463
www.blueskyvineyard.com

The Blue Sky Winery is a bit difficult to find, but very much worth the effort. Hey, you are on a road trip, who cares if you have to rough it a bit instead of gliding to the local wine shop to "pick up a few essentials?" You now have no excuse for not driving over there!

*

I cannot remember my first trip to West Virginia; it was probably in the back of the family Rambler station wagon. What I do know is that the place is beautiful. John Denver was right when he made a song about it. "Almost heaven, West Virginia…"

Anyway, I was motoring along on a trip to Baltimore on Interstate 79/ Interstate 68 in northern West Virginia. (It sounds funny to be calling the northern of something that starts with West.) Those freeways meet in Morgantown. Probably a wonderful little town, but I haven't stopped to inquire from the Chamber of Commerce.

My trusty automobile once again veered off the freeway at the notification that a winery was nearby.

The sign lied! Lied like a dog in front of the fireplace!

Twice I slowed down to rethink the idea, as I drove further and further away from the Interstate. Did it say the winery was two miles away? Wasn't that three miles ago? Is any part of the road straight!

As I got closer to the winery, I began to see signs that also advertised a distillery of the same name. "Hmmm, this is either going to be very interesting or very disappointing."

Not being familiar with the West Virginia sense of humor, this could be an Escher drawing designed to confuse me until I was out of gas! Everywhere farms and woods, not a hint of a vineyard.

Just as I was pretty much tired of this game, I crested a small rise and on the left was a sign saying, "Tasting Room" on an old white building.

Mumbling to myself, "This better be worth all of this harassment!"

My car had turned off the freeway all by its own self, (I'm sure you understand.) The only reason I had continued this charade of crazy roads was the name of the winery. You have to have something to offer if your establishment is the, "Forks of Cheats Winery." Cheats? As in, "I cheated on Solitaire and still lost!" Really, 'cheats'?

I was still a bit miffed (British Standard for mildly annoyed) when I opened the door, entering what must have once been a small home. Rather antique-ish in décor, but I wasn't there to look for an influence by Frank Lloyd Wright, but rather to see if the place knew how to make wine. I wasn't being cheated by the Forks of Cheat, was I?

I quickly got an education!

Now remember, this is a book on why you should consider getting your lazy fanny off the couch and discover the unheard-of winery down the road, not why wine snobs are the way they are. (I may explain that at another time, if you aggravate me enough!)

I had never heard of a Seyval Blanc grape. Later I found out that everyone else on the planet already knew about it and my ignorance was not my most redeeming feature.

What I quickly found out about their Seyval Blanc is that there are no residual sugars in the wine. 0.00%. Yes, that is pretty close to none. I can't say that about their other white wines, but I really liked this one. I unloaded a few bottles from their inventory, along with a few of their Merlots and Cabernet Sauvignons, both of which are very low on residual sugars.

I had been eyeing the distillery products piled up on a nearby shelf.

Rum, moonshine and grappa!

Okay, rum I can understand, though it has nothing to do with wine. Rum is a by-product of sugar cane processing.

Moonshine? Commercial production? I have found the good moonshine comes from North Carolina and you should only drink it if the producer does it as an art form. There is a huge difference between someone trying to make a truck load of money with a cheap 'still' and someone who demands that his moonshine is the best he can make.

The peach moonshine I have had in North Carolina is so smooth, never burning and it will quietly knock your butt in the dirt! That is the only fair warning you will ever get, so underline it and dog-ear the page!

Back to item number three: Grappa!

Have you ever seen the bumper stickers with the words, "Just say NO!"? The next time you see that bumper sticker, consider it is in reference to grappa. Come on, it is the junk they scraped out of the wine vats! You really don't need that stuff!

But then, there are people who like it, though I have no interest in finding out why.

If your television is in the repair shop, or if you happen to be near Morgantown, a stop to this winery would be worthwhile. I strangled my GPS when I got back in my car for making me drive all over the place when in reality it was only about 3 miles away from the freeway.

It ignored me, just like it always does.

Forks of Cheat Winery
2811 Stewartstown Road
Morgantown, WV 26508
(304) 598-2019
www.wvwines.com

Oh, 'Cheat' is the name of the river and I think the nearby lake. So, they are on the fork of the Cheat River.

I picked up a bottle of their rum, too. It is still unopened. Maybe, I'll send it to Sylvia at Luna Rosa in Deming! I bet she could make tiramisu with it!

*

If you are close enough to the Forks of Cheat Winery, you aren't that far away from another surprising find: Knob Hall Winery.

Now their name is not as catchy as the 'cheaters' down the road, but they are definitely worth the effort to find.

The wine tasting room must be an old hay barn. Ignore all of that if ambience is what interests you in a wine. To me the fancier the wine tasting room, the more I wonder if they are hiding something. I like it to be nice, but the Taj Mahal is in India.

I was driving in a bit of a hurry, more than normal, as I expected them to close early on a Sunday. I lucked out. In more than one way! They were open!

Another notch on my educational belt, as I discovered a red wine that was designed to be drank refrigerator cold! (Most of the dead wine snobs are now rolling over in their graves, but so what?)

My attention was quickly grabbed when I saw the label on a different red wine. "Jealous Mistress" reminds me of my 'other girlfriend,' Jessica Rabbit! (Sorry Roger, now you know the truth. I tried to hide it from you.)

Often a catchy label is about the best you can expect from the wine. This is not the case with Jealous Mistress. This is a rather nice wine in my humble opinion.

I also liked their Willow and White Oak for white wines. The other red I tried, and bought, was N39. A strange name, but it has to do with the latitude that the grapes were grown in. They said it was still in 'bottle shock', after asking me if I knew what that was! Duh, I think so.

There is a great movie by that name, *Bottle Shock* and I highly recommend watching it. I doubt if the French watch it, since it explains how they got…. Well, I shouldn't tell you. It is NOT the same as, *Sideways* the other wine movie that more people are familiar with. *Bottle Shock* is a true story.

If I were to complain about anything about Knob Hall Winery, is their staff shouldn't be selling wine unless they enjoy it. Be happy when I show up, please! Even if the happiest time is when I leave! No one seemed to be excited that they were working at a wonderful winery. Forgive them, for they know not that they are surrounded by greatness.

Two cases of wine later, I was headed to Fredrick, MD. Well, actually, 25 bottles. I decided I liked their wine enough that I picked up another bottle to share with friends. Their information is:

Knob Hall Winery
14108 St. Paul Road
Clear Spring, MD 21722
(301) 842-2777
www.knobhallwinery.com

*

23

All of the wineries that I listed I found by accident. (Ignoring the automatic turning device my old Pinto seems to have acquired.) None of them have endorsed this book, but then I haven't asked them. It is a surprise!

Junction Rivers Winery: I needed fuel and something other than dried up chicken.

Charlie Curry Winery: I parked my wife at his tasting room while I checked out an old hotel.

St. Clair Winery: Just happened to be in the right place and the right time.

Luna Rosa Winery: They had a sign! Do you need any other excuse, oops, I mean reason, to stop?

All of the Finger Lakes wineries I found out of curiosity. I knew they were there, I just didn't know they were so good.

Blue Sky Winery: I can say the never-ending Illinois road construction may have had something to do with it.

Forks of Cheat Winery: The name attracted me out of curiosity, but it may have been the fault of my car in collusion with my GPS.

Knob Hall Winery: Who would think of Maryland for wines? By the way, they have more than you would think.

The point is I couldn't have found any of these places if I hadn't been willing to look. There have been a few wineries I drove by and I wish I had stopped, while I have not listed some of the places I shouldn't have bothered.

If you are adventurous but not quite the wanderlust like I am, the other great option is traveling the internet.

www.wineweb.com is a great site, as it shows wineries by state and region. You would be surprised to find a winery might be right around the corner from you. While I was researching that website, I found out that there are two wineries almost within walking distance from my

24

house, but I didn't know they were there! Here I have been driving all around all over the place, and I didn't know they were there. Now, I don't know if they are any good, but hey, there is only one way to find out!

Where is my trusty steed?

WHERE TO FIND 'HORRIBLE' WINE ON THE ROAD

This is where I can be getting myself in big trouble! I mean BIG trouble!

Should I list the places I have been to that I wouldn't recommend to a man dying from dehydration?

In the elusive search for the next surprising winery, you have to willing to know when to leave a winery's tasting room when there is nothing that impresses you.

I recently had that exact experience. All of their wines were sweeter than your old Aunt Bee. I know there are many people who like sweet wines; I'm just not one of them. That is why I wasn't interested in the Finger Lakes Rieslings, knowing the German version is too sweet for me. It was in New York that I learned the Riesling can be made in a drier version.

Now is a good time to ask about dry versus sweet.

Dry wine? Is that like powdered wine? Why do they call one wine, dry, while the next wine is labeled, sweet? Why not say sweet and not sweet? When you think about it, not sweet just doesn't sound right, but neither does calling a wine you know is wet, dry.

Very confusing. The best thing is to ask the winery if they have wines of the type you are interested in sampling, explaining whether you like a sweet wine or not. They really don't care; they are in the business of introducing and showing off their wines. They are not there to convince you of the errors of your ways.

If you get too involved in the terminology of wine, you are slowly moving to the Dark Side of Snobbery! I'm trying to keep you on the Right Path by nudging you away from the technical part of wine, and instead recommending the adventure of Wine Snooping.

The retched wine snobs, left pinky finger permanently extended, can take all of the fun out of wine.

Don't let them get near you, as they will suck all of the happiness out of a room, faster than Dracula can drain your blood.

Though I don't recommend walking around with a wooden stake in your hand while tasting wine, mentally you might want to keep it in mind. And to make you worry a little bit more, they live nearby. There is always a "wanna-be wine snob" in the neighborhood.

Back to the recent unimpressive winery, I did find they had a very surprising Seyval Blanc carbonated wine. So even the worse can be worth considering. The fact that they were connected to a truck stop should have been my first clue. I only bought one bottle, and when I got home and shared it with my wife. She looked at me in wonder.

"Why did you only buy one bottle?" she asked.

*

With around 9,000 wineries in the United States, a number that is growing every day, there is bound to be a few wineries that are not worth talking about. You have to willing to take the few bad with the many good. Never give up on wine exploration because of a few lousy wineries. Most of the great wineries started out making junk! In fact, probably all of them did at one point. It wasn't until they realized their mistakes did they change things. On occasion, even the great winery you went to last year has a bad production.

It is The Quest and The Adventure that you are after, not the snobbery!

RED VS WHITE
(None of that pink stuff, thank you very much!)

First, I am not a good 'Club Member' kind of a guy. I have enough credit cards and trying to keep track of another membership does not interest me.

If you are going to buy a case of wine from a winery, you should insist on some sort of a discount. If they do not offer it, ask. Money is money.

The more you buy, the more you should be able to negotiate. Two cases of anything should get you the 'club membership' discount without having to agree to the normal installment plan they try to sell you on. The answer is, "No!"

I want them to be in business when I want more wine, but why shouldn't I get a decent deal when I am buying more than the average guy on the other end of the tasting room? If you have friends with you, bundle your purchases to get the discount.

With two cases you should be able to get a 20% discount. Don't expect to get much more than that. You want them to be in business when you return for more, but someone has to pay for the gasoline in the Old Pinto, and you might as well take it out of the profits.

I am sure none of my favorite winery owners will read this book, so I'm off the hook on this one.

Remember, if you save the discount money, you can buy more wine!

Here comes the confusing part. You know Merlot is a red wine, right? Well, I thought so until I came along a white Merlot. How do you make a white wine out of a red one? You can't! They are suckering you into a pink wine, so be careful!

Now, if you like pink wines, the white merlot might be your sip of choice.

Red wines are made from black or dark colored grapes, while white wine is made from the light colored ones, such as green grapes.

What more do you need to know? Dark equals red, light equals white. Ignore the pink stuff which can be very confusing.

I hope everyone likes wine in a different way. My tastes are mine, while yours should be yours. The illusive search for the next winery may bring you to Nirvana, so never give up on changing taste buds.

Red wines typically last longer in the bottle. If you open the bottle, try to drink it within twenty four hours. If you know it will be another day before you can finish it, then try putting it in the refrigerator for the night and warm it back prior to draining the bottle down your throat. There is no guarantee it will last the third day, but if it was a nice wine, why waste it?

The reds also last longer unopened, but you need to keep them out of extreme heat. If your house has a place that is typically cooler all the time, then try storing them there. If you live out on the desert, you have a few options. One, drink it now! Two, buy a little wine refrigerator. Some are specifically made for red wines. This limits the number of bottles you can have at one time, but that is much better than ruining your stock.

Some red wines have lasted for hundreds of years, and some are extremely expensive. I wonder if they are better as a curiosity than a drinkable fluid. How does anyone know if the stuff is any good?

I have read that a 3,700 year old wine cellar had been found in the Middle East, but who is drinking it?

Aging your wine can be a tricky business. If you are into saving wine for decades, you might want to find an authority to help you. I personally have a few nice red wines that I should drink, but I fear some of them are turning into vinegar. With so many nice wines to try, the older ones have a tendency to get dusty.

Oh, speaking of dusty wine! My first experience with a Syrah almost gagged me! It made me think I was drinking something that had been strained through a vacuum cleaner bag! I was at a nice dinner in Apple Valley, California and I didn't know much about wine. While everyone was oohing and aahing about the wine, I was looking at them as if they had all lost their minds! No one had the courage (including me, I suppose) to tell the host the wine had been filtered by the maid's Hoover!

Fast forward a few years and Charlie Curry had a Syrah that I tentatively tried, knowing what I would expect. Not the dusty vacuum cleaner bag wine that I was anticipating, and after that I have found quite a few Syrahs that are very decent.

It just shows you that you have to be willing to try a wine again.

Most, or all, wines have sulfites in them. If you have a very mild reaction to sulfites, I would recommend staying with white wines. Often the wine maker will add sulfites to the wine as an additional preservative. You can also look on the bottle label and see if they have a notice, "sulfites added," or "contains sulfites".

Wine production used to be a really hit-or-miss operation. Here comes another history lesson.

Louis Pasteur discovered that heating the wine during part of the production cycle would kill the micro-organisms that caused some wines to go rancid. In the past, you only found out if you had bad wine when the fermentation period was over and you had let it age. An entire year's production could be ruined and sometimes the lost was unrecoverable, destroying a business and the livelihood of the family.

Fast forward, wine is still pasteurized, but now they may add sulfites as an added precaution. There are naturally occurring sulfites in wine, so you are not going to find many wines that are 'sulfite-free' but there are a few. An easy internet search will let you know if there are any wines with zero sulfites available in your area. There are many people who have a serious reaction to sulfites, so please keep this precaution in mind.

Sulfites are related to the natural element Sulfur. (Remember that funny Table of Elements thing the science teacher had on the wall? Yeah, that's it.) Knowing there are sulfite-free wines available, it allows those who have an allergic reaction to still enjoy wine.

*

White wine typically does not last long, compared to a red. If you buy a case of that great tasting white wine you found on your accidental journey, ask the winery how long they expect it to keep. They usually can tell you within a few-months range, knowing their wines from experience. It has been my understanding that their timeline is shorter than I find it to be, but perhaps they are being more cautious.

Yes, I have had to pour out a few bottles because I thought I knew more than the winemaker.

If a white wine is clear and clean, you are probably okay. If it starts getting a tint of brown, you might be in trouble. So watch your wines.

If a white wine tastes funny, pour it out! Don't even bother with it. I have tried turning it into Sangria, and only once in a while will that work. Did you want fruit in your wine? I didn't think so. If you are going to make Sangria, use a nice wine. Not a fantastic wine, but never a bad wine.

If your white fine is fizzy and it is not Champagne (sparkling wine) then it is going towards the drain in your sink. Fizzy wine actually likes it when you feed it to the drain, so give it what it wants.

If the cork in the wine bottle is pushing out on its own, then you can add that to the list of fizzy wine headed down you-know-where.

Any wine that doesn't smell or taste right, probably isn't.

*

Once in a while you will find a bottle of wine with a really great label! If you found it at the winery, then you might be okay. If you found it at the curio shop down the street, then think of it as a fancy bottle. Either drink it right away, or consider it a perfect gift to the annoying wine snob who works in your office.

That reminds me, I have two bottles I need to send to the Original Trailer Park Lounge and Grill on 271 W 23rd Street in New York. Someone remind me!

If you happen to be in the area, it is a great little place filled with more nostalgia than the Spam Museum in Austin, Minnesota.

*

Champagne! That intentionally fizzy stuff!

The true story about how Champagne was discovered is extremely bland and not worth telling, and no one probably really knows that tale. The myth far exceeds the truth to the point that who cares? It is a great myth and everyone should hear it.

I was told that a blind 17th century monk, Dom Perignon, started it all. That he was blind and still the cellar master is difficult to understand. He was making wine and found out that his production had gone bad, all of it was fizzy. Remember, fizzy can mean the wine has gone bad.

Rather than pour out the whole lot, including his job at the vineyard, he is said to have come up with a brilliant sales pitch. Convincing everyone that he had discovered something wonderful, he said, "Come quickly, my brothers! I am drinking stars!"

Probably saved many a relationship with his discovery, too!

I have a tough time with Champagne. I like it, but I can't understand how a two hundred dollar bottle of fizz is worth so much!

How can a 1993 Dom Perignon be worth from a drop bottom price of $74, up to $747, a ten-fold price range? Or a year 2000 can be worth $360?

How can a Louis Roederer Cristal also have a ten-fold price range of $24 to $240?

My biggest problem is that what I like the most every Champagne snob (much higher elevated than the average old wine snob) would shun with disgust.

I like Weibel's 'Almondage'. It is almond- flavored Champagne that cost less than ten bucks, if I can get it. You can get almond flavored Champagnes, here and there, but I like this one the best. Most people have never heard of them, so if you are curious, try it.

If I find that my Almondage becomes unavailable because I have been blabbering about it, I will shred this book! Yes, you may buy a bottle or two, but don't start buying it by the case, because I don't want to drive all over town looking for it when my stock gets low.

There are many debates and legal issues that surround the use of the word, "Champagne." The very short version: California has the right, while most other areas cannot. Champagne is a region in France and the word is protected in the Versailles Treaty ending World War One. The French are a bit picky about this, you know. Even after Texas saved their wine industry!

GRAPES!

I have a single grape vine trying its best to survive the Houston summer. I was told that if I have more than one vine, it qualifies as a vineyard.

There are wine grapes and then there are table grapes.

Table grapes are typically bigger and fatter. They are easy to eat; many of them have no seeds. They usually are less sweet and have less acid than wine grapes.

Wine grapes on the other hand, are pretty much the reverse of the table variety. Little round things that you can eat, but it will not take long before you realize the need to stay with the table grapes. They are too sweet, full of acid and are sometimes a mess to eat.

If table grapes were wine producers, the world would be covered in wine. So don't go to the grocery store and buy fifty pounds of table grapes and think you are in the wine business.

If you knew how little the winemaker gets out of a grape, you would find more appreciation for his craft. You have to pound a serious amount of grapes to get a bottle of wine. Some wineries will allow you to see the process, under very tight supervision. If you get a chance, take it. Only then will you realize the ratio of grape-to-wine that they have to deal with.

Most wineries sell off the bulk 'trash' to local farmers, keeping their operation as profitable as possible.

Not all wine grapes are destined to be wine.

Brandy is distilled wine. That is why some moonshiners refer to their liquor as brandy if they are using something other than grain in their mash. Brandy is a wine that has much higher alcohol content due to the distilling process.

Cognac is brandy with a fancier name. According to the Dutch it is still burnt wine. I think the word Cognac may also require a higher price on the bottle.

Then, there is vinegar.

I won't get into the vinegar story, but if you ever get a chance to try vinegar tasting (sounds awful, I know) do it. There are so many types of vinegar, some of which are actually quite nice. No one is going to ask for a glass of vinegar, but the health benefits are unbelievable. There are a few vinegar tasting rooms, dotted here and there. If you are interested in something very different on your road trip, this might be it.

*

The types of grapes relate to the type of wine that is produced.

When you read the label on a wine bottle, it should tell you what kinds of grapes were used. It could be a specific grape variety or a blend of others. Some of the nicest wines are blends, so do not stick your nose up to them. It helps you avoid the nasty wine-snobbery attitude.

*

"Texas saves the French wine industry!" Banner news if you lived in the 1880's.

Europe's wine industry was devastated by a root disease that wiped out 80% of their crops. A guy named Thomas Volney Munson, who lived in Denison, Texas near Dallas, was perhaps one of the biggest authorities on grapes and vines. His book is still considered required reading in winemaking school. (That is 'Oenology' in case you are wondering.)

The French contacted him. He saved their industry and got the French Legion of Honor Chevalier du Mérite Agricole. Fancy words for "Thank you for saving our bacon!"

Here it gets a bit sticky! Does this mean that the French wine is really Texas wine? You can say that in

Texas, but I wouldn't recommend trying it on the other side of the pond. The French police have no sense of humor!

TO STASH OR NOT TO STASH, THAT IS THE QUESTION

If you have the room in either your house or your wallet, piling up a nice collection of wine can be a great diversion. It doesn't have to be very expensive.

Getting someone to build a wine room for you can be more difficult than running around the country buying wine from the vineyards. One of the ways is to find someone on the internet who sells wine racks and build your own. The good part of that is you can add it to something you already have. It can be anything you want it to be: a whole room, or a less-used closet in a spare bedroom. Your imagination can go wild with the possibilities. As for the spare bedroom, you needed to clean that thing out anyway.

Once you have a wine room, it is amazing how soon you will find friends who are either interested in donating to your collection, or helping you taste the ones you have. It is great to be able to hunt the right wine to bring to a party when you know you have a wide selection that no one is familiar with. Bringing a wine from some hole-in-the-wall winery with an explanation about how you found the place is very different than running down to the local liquor store and picking a bottle you know is 'safe.'

With the wine racks in place, you can label the rows with the different wineries, states or whether they are red or white.

As for whether you should stash your wine or not is up to you. If you live in a wine producing region, having a pile of wine seems wasteful.

But then, what happens if the area has a drought and the price of wine goes sky-high? You don't need to stock wine unless you are either a collector or a serious wine drinker. The only other reason is because you want to!

It is fun to have a 'wine tasting party' with friends. Try a Champagne tasting event after you have acquired enough different bottles. You can integrate your wine stash into a cooking class. I have a world-class chef who may not be impressed with my kitchen, but I guarantee that there is a wine she has never tried sitting on one of my racks. (Yes, that is you, Kelly!) You can find her at:

www.eventplanningbooks.net

Back to cooking, there are many recipes that require wine. I usually wonder about that. Are you supposed to drink the wine or pour it in the bowl? Try both, just to make sure the food is right.

*

Trying to understand wine snobbery is sometimes like trying to herd cats. Give it a try and let me know how successful you are.

They are arrogant and impatient. They are intolerant of mere mortals. They have been culled out the rest of mankind to create a super-race of beings with senses that we lower churls are unable to understand. Yes, just like cats.

You can always see them trying to demean someone by their expertise.

"You don't know the difference from a 1951 vintage Blah-blah-blah and a 1958 vintage Nit-pick-blanc? Tsk, tsk. How dreadful."

Ya know what I know? A wine I like! I hope you can find the wines that you like in your expeditions of finding the unknown wineries around the turn in the bend.

The whole idea of this book is to motivate you to think about trying something new, and not from the liquor store shelf, though I agree that is easier.

How many weekends have you totally forgotten what you did all day? How many trips have you taken and can't remember a single thing about the journey?

Get out and be wild! The age limitation on being crazy is rather wide open.

If you don't like wine, I doubt if you bought this book. If you need ideas of where to go, the internet is a good place to start. Your local AAA (as opposed to AA, keep them separate) may have a local wine region map and they are very helpful.

Ask friends! They may want to go with you. Of course, they will want to drink up your wine, so be careful.

Always enjoy life! That is what wine was made for!

IN THE END

The great part is that you can't do it wrong. Whether you decide on traveling to a known winery, or just pull off the road when you see a winery sign, you just can't do it wrong.

It is the excuse for an adventure that may lead you to places you never knew existed.

I have been blessed in being able to drive around our wonderful country and this is my way of trying to share that blessing with you. I cannot tell you how many times I was in such a rush to get somewhere, only to find that I was too early or things had been canceled.

Don't be in such a panic that you forget to enjoy your life. If your life is so structured that you don't have time to have fun, what is the purpose? The true purpose in life is to enjoy it.

It is very difficult to have a bad day with a good glass of wine in your hand!

It's time to start planning your next wine journey!

Dennis
Contact me:
dennisvalder@aol.com

Made in the USA
San Bernardino, CA
30 July 2014